AN
ELEPHANT
IS SOFT
AND
MUSHY

D1569161

Other Avon Books by
S. Gross

I Am Blind And My Dog Is Dead

AN
ELEPHANT
IS SOFT
AND
MUSHY

CARTOONS BY
S. GROSS

 AVON
PUBLISHERS OF BARD, CAMELOT, DISCUS AND FLARE BOOKS

I am indebted to the following Copyright owners for permission to reprint cartoons owned by them:
Of the 118 drawings in this collection, 11 originally appeared in *The New Yorker* and were
   Copyrighted © 1977, 1978, and 1979 by *The New Yorker* magazine, Inc.
Cartoons on pages 8/9, 15, 19, 20/21, 22, 23 *top*, 24, 25, 28, 30, *top*, 32/33, 35, 38, 42, 44/45, 46, 50, 51,
   53, 54, 55, 56/57, 58/59, 63, 64, 66/67, 68, 70, 72 *bottom* 73, 74, 79 *top*, 91, 94, 98/99, 101, 107, 109,
   110/111, 113, 114 *top*, 115 *top*, 119 *top*, 120, 121, 122/123, 124 *top*, and 126/127 reprinted with
   permission of *National Lampoon* magazine.
Cartoons on pages 7, 10 *top* and *bottom*, 11, 12/13, 17 *bottom*, 26 *top*, 29, 30 *bottom*, 40 *top*, 49, 52
   bottom, 60, 65, 71, 90, 96, 100, 106, 124, and 125 reprinted by permission of the Chicago
   Tribune-New York Syndicate, Inc.
Cartoons on pages 48, 78, 92/93, and 104/105 originally appeared in *Esquire* magazine.
   Copyright © 1969, 1970 by Esquire, Inc. Copyright © 1977 by Esquire magazine, Inc.
Cartoons on pages 62 and 112 *top* reprinted from *CAVALIER* magazine.
Cartoons on pages 79 *bottom* and 128 are courtesy of *Good Housekeeping* magazine.
Cartoons on pages 16 and 116/117 *bottom* Copyright © 1976, 1979 by The New York Times
   Company. Reprinted by permission.
Cartoons on pages 34 and 72 *top* reprinted from *Saturday Review.*
Cartoon on page 14 reprinted with permission from *Changing Times*, February 1978 issue.
Cartoon on page 85 reprinted with permission of *Cosmopolitan* magazine.
Cartoon on page 80/81 reproduced by special permission of *OUI.* Copyright © 1974 by Playboy
   Pubs., Inc.
Cartoon on page 47 Copyright © by *The Washington Post.*
Grateful acknowledgement is also made to the following publications in whose pages single
   cartoons reprinted in this book first appeared: *High Times, Medical Opinion & Review,* and
   National Enquirer.

This book's first cartoon appears on page 7.

Cover illustration by S. Gross.

AVON BOOKS
A division of
The Hearst Corporation
959 Eighth Avenue
New York, New York 10019

Copyright © 1980 by S. Gross
Published by arrangement with Dodd, Mead & Company
Library of Congress Catalog Card Number: 79-28642
ISBN: 0-380-57679-1

The Dodd, Mead & Company edition contains the following Library of Congress Cataloging in
Publication Data:

Gross, Sam.
   An elephant is soft and mushy.

   1. American wit and humor, Pictorial. I. Title.
NC1429.G76A4   1980   741.5'973   79-28642

First Avon Printing, May, 1982

For Michelle

S. GROSS

"Romulus is going to found Rome and Remus is going into municipal bonds."

S.GROSS

"Just one more question. Do you have any medical insurance?"

S.GROSS

"Of course I couldn't have ever done it without my new microwave oven."

"Welchen Weg zum Metropolitan Opern Haus?"

S.GROSS

"I had a wet dream last night."

S.GROSS

S. GROSS

S. GROSS

"An old lady <u>used</u> to live there. Now it's a Montessori school."

"Whatever you do, don't default on your loan."

S.GROSS

"Well . . . the kiss didn't work. How about a blow job?"

S.GROSS

"Three hard-ons."

S. GROSS

FALLING
COMMANDMENT
ZONE

S.GROSS

"Who is it?"

"If you don't mind me saying so, this is the lousiest caning I've ever received."

"Forgive me for staring, but I never saw a Snoopy diaphragm before."

S.GROSS

S. GROSS

S. G

"Now do you believe me, darling? There's the proof that it does turn black and eventually falls off."

"Can I use your bathroom?"

S.GROSS

"We thought a nice little birdie would cheer you up."

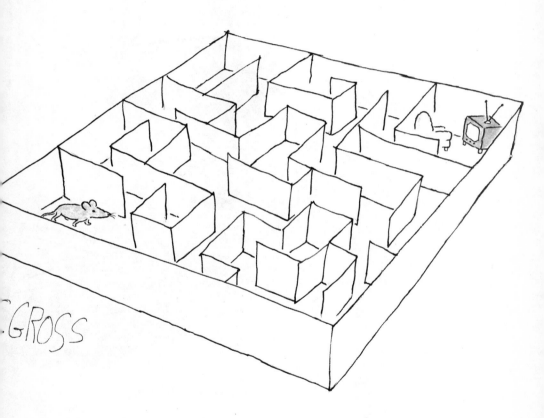

GROSS

"Look out. It's Manbat!"

S.GROSS

"Now cough!"

S.GROSS

"It's a little trick I learned. You just squeeze their balls."

"We <u>know</u> it was the Gingerbread Boy! We found crumbs in her vagina."

S.GROSS

"What's the catch?"

"You owe me 2,640,000 dollars. That hotel has a casino."

"Hello, is this Miss Davis the nursery school teacher? This is an obscene phone call, Miss Davis, Ca-ca, poo-poo, sissie, tushy, boom-boom . . ."

"Naturally curly hair."

S. GROSS

S.GROSS

S.GROSS

S. GROSS

"Bad news, fellas. Her medical insurance ran out."

"Tell the chef, no more frozen pies."

S. GROSS

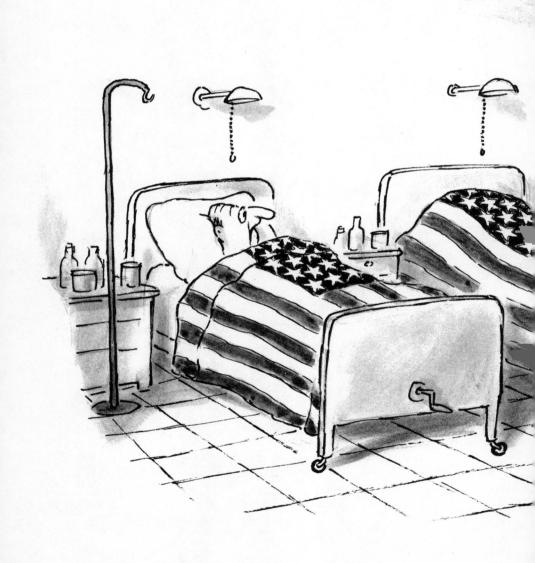

"It's the only way I can get it to stay on."

BUY
A
PENCIL

"Hey, I've had it with winding you! From here on in you're going to
have to make it on your own."

Medusa in a Dublin bar after St. Patrick chased
the snakes out of Ireland.

"Tomorrow morning you will be found frozen to death."

S. GROSS

"Fongu!"

"Have you had any previous banking experience?"

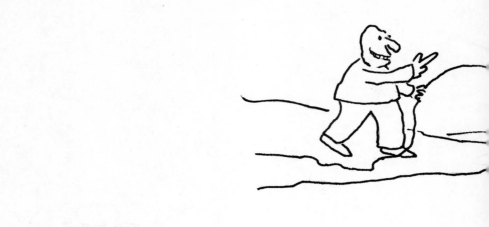

"Did you know that 'getting fixed' means having your balls cut off?"

S.GROSS

"So far all they've done was come and put up that sign."